JACK REACHER BOOKS, NOVELLA'S & SHORT STORIES

IN PUBLICATION AND CHRONOLOGICAL ORDER

THE DEFINITIVE GUIDE:

(INCLUDES TV & FILM ADAPTATIONS)

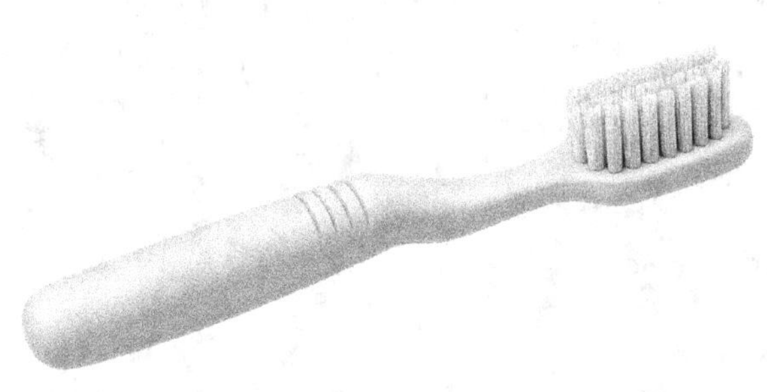

Contents

1. LEE CHILD: THE MAN WHO BUILT A LITERARY GIANT WITH A TOOTHBRUSH AND A TEMPER — 1

2. ANDREW CHILD: THE QUIET BROTHER WHO TOOK ON JACK REACHER AND KEPT HIM STANDING — 7

3. THE MAN WHO WALKS: AN UNCIVILISED LOOK AT JACK REACHER — 13

4. JACK REACHER BOOKS IN ORDRE OF PUBLICATION — 20

5. JACK REACHER BOOKS IN CHRONOLOGICAL ORDER — 49

6. PUBLICATION ORDER OF JACK REACHER SHORT STORIES — 52

7. PUBLICATION ORDER OF JACK REACHER COLLECTIONS — 63

8. JACK REACHER QUIZ: 20 QUESTIONS — 66

9. JACK REACHER ON SCREEN: FROM   68
    MISCAST BLOCKBUSTER TO PRIME
    REDEMPTION

10. JACK REACHER QUIZ ANSWERS   75

LEE CHILD: THE MAN WHO BUILT A LITERARY GIANT WITH A TOOTHBRUSH AND A TEMPER

If you were writing Jack Reacher's origin story, you might start with a man being sacked in his forties and thinking, "Right then—I'll write a novel." That man, improbably and gloriously, is Lee Child. Born Jim Grant in Coventry in 1954 and raised in the concrete slopes of Birmingham, Lee Child didn't so much stumble into thriller writing as stride into it, six foot five, fists clenched, and quietly furious.

But let's rewind a bit.

THE BRUMMIE BEGINNING

Lee Child's early years weren't littered with guns or car chases, but they were rich in books and imagination. The second of four brothers, he grew up with a strong moral compass and a deep love for story—particularly the kind that involves justice being served. At school, he was clever, bookish, and fascinated by narrative structure. He went on to study law at the University of Sheffield, which he didn't particularly enjoy, but it gave him a solid foundation in logic, language, and the strange workings of human behaviour—all useful tools for someone who'd go on to make a living writing about moral dilemmas with body counts.

STAGE LEFT: BROADCASTING

Before becoming a global bestselling author, Jim Grant spent nearly 20 years at Granada Television in Manchester, where he worked as a presentation director. If you watched TV in the North in the 1980s and early 90s, odds are he cued up your ad breaks. He also worked on everything from live football to Prime Suspect, earning a solid reputation as a cool-headed, creative professional. But in 1995, after a corporate shake-up, he was made redundant.

Most people, when handed a redundancy cheque, worry about the mortgage. Child went out and bought a pad of paper and some pencils.

He later said he'd been preparing for that moment his whole life.

THE BIRTH OF REACHER

The story goes that Child started writing his first novel, Killing Floor, out of a sort of quiet rage. He was 40, unemployed, and suddenly in possession of too much time and not enough money. So he sat down and created a character who was everything he admired: tough, clever, moral, physically imposing, and entirely unbothered by modern life. Jack Reacher was born—ex-military police, no home, no luggage, no nonsense.

Killing Floor was published in 1997 and was an instant hit. It won the Anthony Award for Best First Novel and introduced readers to a new kind of thriller hero: a man with no roots, no fear, and no patience for bullies.

What followed was nothing short of a publishing phenomenon.

THE REACHER FORMULA (WITHOUT FEELING FORMULAIC)

Reacher books follow a comforting rhythm. Reacher arrives in a new town, something dodgy happens, and before long there are bodies, broken noses, and a growing sense that someone's about to learn a hard lesson. But within that structure, Child plays with setting, tone, and theme. Some are locked-room mysteries. Others are political thrillers. Some have the slow-burn mood of noir, while others are all-out action romps.

What unites them all is Reacher himself—stoic, principled, and often the smartest man in the room (though he'd never say so). He's a loner who doesn't want trouble, but will happily end it when it appears. He's got the instincts of a philosopher and the reach of a heavyweight boxer.

And through Reacher, Lee Child created a literary voice that's stripped-down, clean, and effortlessly readable. Short sentences. Sharp dialogue. No flab.

Child has often said he deliberately broke the rules of traditional writing. He starts sentences with "and" and "but." He ends chapters with hooks designed to keep you up past your bedtime. And it works—millions of readers later, Reacher remains one of the most borrowed, bought, and binge-read characters in fiction.

FAME, FORTUNE, AND ONE VERY BIG SHADOW

By the time Child had written a dozen Reacher books, he was a global name. The novels were translated into over forty languages. They sold more than 100 million copies. At one point, a Reacher novel was being sold every nine seconds.

And then came Hollywood.

In 2012, Tom Cruise was cast as Reacher in the film adaptation of One Shot, and later in Never Go Back. Fans were baffled. Reacher is famously 6'5", built like a fridge, and described in nearly every book as physically intimidating. Cruise, while a capable actor and no stranger to action, didn't fit the bill. Child defended the casting, saying Cruise had the "presence" to carry it off, but quietly admitted that readers had a point.

The Amazon Prime series rebooted things in 2022 with Alan Ritchson—taller, broader, and much more Reacher-ish—and fans rejoiced.

Despite the fame, Child stayed grounded. He was known for his kindness to fans, his dry humour, and his curious blend of aloofness and warmth. He smoked like a chimney, wrote standing up, and claimed never to plan his books in advance—he'd just start with a sentence and see where it led. He once called it "the novelist's equivalent of tightrope walking without a net."

THE COLLABORATION: ENTER ANDREW

In 2020, after writing 24 Reacher books solo, Child decided to hand over the reins to someone he trusted completely—his younger brother, Andrew Grant, who'd already carved out a respectable career as a thriller writer under his own name. He would now write as "Andrew Child."

The plan was a smooth handover. They'd co-author a few books—starting with The Sentinel in 2020—before Andrew took the lead fully. The tone shifted slightly under this new pairing: the plots got faster, the tech more modern, the dialogue snappier. Some fans noticed the difference. Others embraced it. Either way, the transition marked the end of one era and the beginning of another.

Lee Child didn't disappear, though. He's still involved in the Reacher universe—advising, shaping, and, you suspect, occasionally tightening a paragraph with that famous editorial ruthlessness.

LEGACY, HABITS, AND A VIEW FROM THE TOP

Lee Child's impact on the thriller genre is huge. He changed the shape of the modern action novel—stripping it down, speeding it up, and giving it a hero who could quote philosophers and snap collarbones without blinking.

His personal writing habits are legendary. He never plans his books. He writes the first draft straight through, never revises, and edits only lightly. He types with two fingers. He claims never to suffer from writer's block because he's always writing toward what he, as a reader, would find interesting.

He's also unusually philosophical for a thriller writer. He's spoken about how Reacher represents a kind of wish fulfilment—a moral force in an increasingly unjust world. He's aware that Reacher's methods are extreme, but argues that they work in fiction because readers know Reacher's heart is in the right place.

And then there's the matter of his name.

"Lee Child" was chosen with shelf visibility in mind. "Child" would sit between "Chandler" and "Christie"—good company. "Lee" was short, punchy, and easy to remember. It worked.

THE MAN BEHIND THE MYTH

Despite the macho world of his books, Lee Child himself is a charming contradiction. He's intellectual, slightly bohemian, and fiercely pro-reader. He's outspoken in defence of libraries and public access to books. He's also refreshingly honest about publishing as a business—he's said, more than once, that writing is a job, and that treating it like one is what helped him succeed.

He now divides his time between New York and the UK, and is often spotted in expensive jackets, usually holding a cigarette and answering questions with a mix of wit, charm, and thinly veiled astonishment that Jack Reacher took off the way he did.

IN CLOSING

Lee Child didn't just write thrillers—he reshaped the landscape. He gave readers a hero who doesn't compromise, doesn't complain, and doesn't carry more than a toothbrush. And through Reacher, he gave himself a second life after redundancy—one that led to global fame, record-breaking sales, and a whole new definition of cool in crime fiction.

He's now stepped back, but not out. Reacher lives on in the hands of his brother. And Lee Child remains a literary legend: the Brummie who built an empire with no plan, no outline, and a bloke who can kill you with a headbutt.

ANDREW CHILD: THE QUIET BROTHER WHO TOOK ON JACK REACHER AND KEPT HIM STANDING

Taking over a bestselling series with over 100 million fans sounds like a brilliant career move until you actually have to do it. That's the job Andrew Child—born Andrew Grant—took on in 2020 when he agreed to carry on the Jack Reacher legacy from his older brother, Lee Child. And not just as a ghostwriter or behind-the-scenes helper, but with his own name on the cover. Sort of.

But who is Andrew Child, and how did he go from relative anonymity to co-piloting one of the biggest franchises in modern fiction?

Andrew Grant was born in 1968 in Birmingham, 14 years after his big brother Jim Grant (who'd later become Lee Child). That age gap meant they weren't just siblings—they were almost from different generations. While Lee was starting out in TV and eventually moving into crime fiction stardom, Andrew was off carving his own path, often far from the spotlight.

He went to school in the Midlands, developed a love for reading early on, and like many younger siblings, had a front-row seat to the rise of a literary giant. But he never seemed intimidated by it. Instead, he quietly watched, listened, and built a creative toolkit of his own.

He studied English Literature and Drama at the University of Sheffield—ironically, the same university where his brother had studied law. Afterwards, Andrew moved into theatre, not novels, forming a production company that staged original plays. It was storytelling from the ground up: tight deadlines, small venues, no safety net. It didn't make him rich, but it taught him how to structure stories, manage tension, and write dialogue that actually sounds like people talking.

Those early theatre years are often overlooked, but they're key to understanding his style—fast-paced, character-driven, and always with a sense of rhythm. He learned how to grab attention quickly, keep it, and leave the audience wanting more. Handy skills for the thriller trade.

After leaving theatre behind, Andrew worked in the corporate world for a while—software, telecoms, the usual suspects. But the creative itch never left him. In the mid-2000s, he decided to try his hand at fiction. His debut novel, Even, was published in 2009 and introduced readers to David Trevellyan, a British intelligence operative with a sardonic wit and a healthy disregard for authority.

The book drew comparisons to Fleming, Ludlum, and—inevitably—his older brother. But Andrew's voice was distinct: punchy, confident, and more international in scope. Even was followed by Die Twice and More Harm Than Good, completing a sharp little trilogy that earned solid reviews and proved that Grant wasn't just cashing in on a famous surname—he had serious chops.

Later came a new character: Paul McGrath, a military man turned vigilante (sound familiar?) who featured in Invisible and Too Close to Home. These were darker, moodier novels, with a strong emotional thread and a tone that showed

Andrew had grown into a writer who understood not just how to thrill, but how to connect.

By this point, he'd married fellow thriller author Tasha Alexander, and they'd settled in Wyoming—one of those wide, dramatic landscapes where you can imagine Reacher walking across the horizon at any moment.

In 2020, after more than two decades of writing Reacher solo, Lee Child announced he was stepping back. He wanted a gentler life—less travel, fewer deadlines, maybe a bit more sleep. But he didn't want Reacher to die with him. And who better to take over than someone with a similar voice, shared DNA, and a proven thriller pedigree?

Andrew Grant became Andrew Child (a publishing decision made to keep the brand unified) and joined his brother on The Sentinel, their first co-written Reacher novel. It was, in effect, a literary baton pass—but instead of a sprint, it would be a three-book relay, easing readers into a new era.

The idea was to preserve what made Reacher so iconic—his wandering spirit, his moral compass, his love of coffee and violence—but to subtly modernise the world around him. Faster plots, more contemporary threats, a bit of tech here and there.

Andrew was respectful of the formula, but not afraid to tinker. Some long-time fans noticed the change immediately: the pace got even faster, the chapters shorter, and the structure more cinematic. Others found it seamless. Either way, the books kept flying off the shelves.

Andrew Child's writing is slicker, more high-octane, and often more plot-driven than his brother's. Where Lee Child built tension with slow reveals and internal monologues, Andrew prefers to keep things moving. You'll find more tech in his books, more complex villain networks, and a slightly more modern feel overall.

But the heart of Reacher remains intact. He still turns up in strange towns, still gets into fights with bad people, and still walks away at the end with nothing but a toothbrush and a clear conscience.

One of Andrew's most impressive achievements is how he's managed to preserve Reacher's voice while gradually reshaping the stories to suit his own style. He didn't do an impression of his brother—he absorbed the rhythm, then added his own beat.

In interviews, he's been refreshingly open about the pressure. He knows how beloved Reacher is. He knows some readers will always prefer "classic" Reacher. But he also knows that keeping a series alive means adapting—and his goal has always been to honour what came before while keeping things fresh.

Since the handover began, Andrew Child has co-authored or written the following Reacher books:

The Sentinel (2020) – the transition book, blending Lee's classic style with Andrew's faster pacing.

Better Off Dead (2021) – darker, more violent, and full of desert paranoia.

No Plan B (2022) – Reacher vs. a shady adoption ring and a conspiracy that spans states.

The Secret (2023) – a return to Reacher's military past, with spy-thriller undertones.

In Too Deep (2024) – classic set-up: small town, big secrets, one-man war on corruption.

Exit Strategy (2025) – upcoming and full of promise, with Reacher drawn into yet another mess just by being in the wrong place at the wrong time.

Each one has felt slightly different, but Reacher's DNA—both literal and figurative—remains.

Andrew's a fairly private figure compared to his brother. He's not all over social media. He doesn't chase interviews. But when he does talk, he comes across as thoughtful, self-aware, and clearly devoted to his craft.

He's spoken about his admiration for Lee's discipline—writing every day, treating it like a job, never waiting for the muse. That ethos has rubbed off. Andrew writes with similar regularity, often standing at his desk, coffee in hand, plotting the next twist.

He's also fiercely respectful of readers. He knows the world is full of distractions, and if someone chooses your book, you owe them something worth their time. That comes through in his writing—tight, focused, and packed with momentum.

And while some critics muttered about "nepotism" when the handover was announced, most now accept that Andrew has proven himself. He's not just keeping the engine running—he's put in a new gearbox and changed the tyres.

Andrew Child is now the full custodian of Jack Reacher, and he seems to be enjoying the challenge. There's talk of pushing the character into new territory—not drastically, but with a keener sense of the modern world. Cybercrime. Surveillance. Smart cities with dumb people. All of it ripe for a man who doesn't carry a phone and doesn't like being watched.

There's also the ongoing Amazon Prime series, which keeps Reacher in the public eye and has brought in a new wave of fans—many of whom are now discovering the books for the first time.

Andrew's job is to balance nostalgia with momentum—to give longtime fans the Reacher they love, while tempting in new readers who want grit, speed, and justice without capes or sci-fi nonsense.

So far, he's doing a damn good job.

Andrew Child might have taken the scenic route to literary fame, but he's earned his place in the Reacher legacy. He's not trying to be Lee. He's not trying to reinvent the wheel. He's just quietly, confidently keeping one of the world's most beloved action heroes alive—and giving him a few new corners to turn.

There's still a long road ahead, and plenty of fights to come. But with Andrew at the wheel, Reacher's future looks just as compelling as his past.

THE MAN WHO WALKS: AN UNCIVILISED LOOK AT JACK REACHER

He walks. That's the first thing. Not rides, not drives, not dials for a cab. Jack Reacher walks. It's not a dramatic walk, either—no slow-motion strut, no booming soundtrack. It's purposeful, calm, and relentless. He walks into town. He walks out. And somewhere in the middle, someone gets thrown through a window.

For over two decades, Jack Reacher has dominated the thriller shelves like a great slab of concrete justice in a denim shirt. He's a former military police major with no home, no phone, and no patience for faff. He owns a toothbrush. He carries it in his pocket. That's about it.

But who is Jack Reacher, really? Why has a man with almost no emotional baggage and zero permanent address become one of the most enduring characters in modern fiction?

Let's dig in.

BIG MAN, BIG MYTH

Physically, Reacher is a tank in human form. Six foot five, 250 pounds, ex-Army muscle, hands like dinner plates. People in the books react to him as if a rhino's just entered the pub. His sheer size is always noted—by shop assistants, waitresses, villains. It's not just a stat—it's a narrative tool. Reacher doesn't need to posture or threaten. He's a walking deterrent.

He drinks black coffee, lots of it. Eats what he can get. Doesn't carry luggage, just buys new clothes every few days and bins the old ones. Lives in the moment. Reads small-town America like a map of pressure points. And when something's wrong, he knows—instinctively, almost mystically.

A LAW UNTO HIMSELF

Reacher's moral code is simple. It goes like this: protect the innocent, punish the guilty, and never hit first unless someone really deserves it.

He's not a lawman. He doesn't care for paperwork, due process, or soft landings. But he's not chaotic either. He's calm, measured, even tender at times. He walks away from arguments unless someone's truly asking for it. He's polite. He respects boundaries. And if someone lays a hand on a woman or a child, or exploits the weak, they will shortly find themselves unconscious or worse.

He's often compared to Western heroes—a lone gunman riding into town to clean it up before disappearing again. But he's also a bit Sherlock Holmes, a bit Clint Eastwood, and a lot of moral fury wrapped in denim.

THE APPEAL: WISH FULFILMENT WITH BRAINS

Let's be honest—there's a strong fantasy element at play here.

Reacher doesn't pay bills. Doesn't worry about jobs, housing, pensions, or flat tyres. He can drop a man twice his size, but he also knows which year the .38 Special was replaced in the NYPD's arsenal. He quotes history, solves crimes, and disappears before anyone can buy him a sandwich.

For readers, he's escapism with intellect. He lives out a kind of justice that we rarely see in real life—swift, clear, and unburdened by bureaucracy. He doesn't compromise. He doesn't waffle. He doesn't tweet.

And yet, he's not cold. He helps strangers. He mourns loss. He gets lonely. He just doesn't show it in ways we're used to.

NO HOME, NO TIES—NO PROBLEM?

One of the most compelling things about Reacher is how little he owns. It's radical. A man who chooses not to accumulate anything—not stuff, not relationships, not regrets. He doesn't want a house. He doesn't have a car. When he stays somewhere overnight, it's usually a motel or a holding cell.

There's something almost monkish about it. Reacher's life is stripped down to the absolute basics: movement, observation, and action. In a world obsessed with clutter and connection, he's off-grid. And that's why people love him.

He makes not caring about conventional success look... sane.

LOVE, ACTUALLY (SORT OF)

Romance isn't central to Reacher's stories, but it's not absent either. He has relationships, often brief and intense. He connects, genuinely, but never sticks around. He's not afraid of love—he just doesn't see the point in staying somewhere when there's nothing left to fix.

That lack of permanence is both romantic and tragic. He's the ultimate "what could have been" figure. And the women in his life tend to be strong, capable, and fully aware of what he is: a storm system passing through, not a foundation to build on.

BRAIN AND BRAWN: THE FULL PACKAGE

It's easy to focus on Reacher's fists (and let's be clear, he uses them a lot), but what really sets him apart is his brain. He notices everything. The layout of a diner. The way someone's shoelace is tied. The timing of a conversation. He unravels conspiracies like a man solving a crossword with his fists.

In almost every book, there's a moment when someone underestimates him. Maybe they think he's just muscle. Maybe they think he's slow. And then he starts talking—quietly, logically, cutting right to the heart of things. It's thrilling. He's not just stronger than the people he's up against—he's smarter. And he knows it.

CHANGING HANDS: FROM LEE TO ANDREW

Reacher was born from Lee Child's brain in 1997, and for over 20 novels, Child maintained a distinctive voice—clean, lean, and surgical. But in 2020, the torch passed to his younger brother Andrew Child (née Grant), who brought a slightly different flavour to the franchise.

The change is subtle, but noticeable. The pacing's quicker. The villains are more digital, the conspiracies more layered. There's a bit more tech, a bit more procedural trickery. But

Reacher's voice remains.

Andrew doesn't try to mimic Lee exactly—he honours the tone while moving the world around Reacher into more modern territory. It's still recognisably Reacher, just with a new coat of paint and maybe a tighter plot structure.

Some fans noticed the difference immediately. Others didn't bat an eye. But the truth is, Reacher himself hasn't changed. He's still the man who'll take down six goons in a bar because someone looked at a waitress the wrong way. And that's what matters.

STANDING STILL, MOVING FORWARD

Despite the passage of time, Reacher doesn't age in the traditional sense. Yes, there are flashbacks and prequels, and yes, we know roughly when he left the Army. But in the current books, he seems forever suspended in his forties—experienced but not creaky, wise but still able to leap from a moving train.

It's a smart move. Like Bond or Batman, Reacher isn't about realism. He's about consistency. We don't want him dealing with arthritis. We want him kicking in doors and quoting Sun Tzu.

That said, there's an increasing sense of weariness in the later books. Not physical fatigue, but emotional. Reacher's seen too much. He's tired of people's selfishness. But instead of growing bitter, he grows more precise. The fights are shorter. The decisions colder. There's a sense that the man is carving deeper into his own myth as he walks.

THE SHAPE OF JUSTICE

Reacher represents a certain kind of justice—immediate,

proportional, and deeply satisfying. In a world where real justice is often delayed or denied, Reacher walks in and sorts it out in 400 pages or less.

He doesn't shoot first, but he never hesitates when it's time to end something. And when he walks away at the end, he leaves behind a slightly better world—and sometimes a few cracked ribs.

This is why readers trust him. Reacher doesn't lie to us. He doesn't change to fit a trend. He just shows up, notices what no one else sees, and does what needs doing.

At the heart of it, Reacher's appeal is simple: he's what we wish we could be. Not just strong or clever, but free. Free from nonsense. Free from bills. Free from bosses. He answers to no one, owes no one, and needs nothing but good shoes and a vague direction.

And yet he cares. That's the kicker. He helps people. Sticks up for the vulnerable. Fights when others can't. He doesn't want thanks. Doesn't want a medal. He just wants to know that, when something went wrong, someone showed up to put it right.

Reacher is the walking embodiment of "if not me, who?"

He's part knight, part detective, part myth. And whether he's penned by Lee or Andrew, whether he's in the desert or the snow, whether he's fighting militia, gangsters, or corrupt feds—he'll always be walking.

Town to town. Trouble to trouble. Justice in his pocket. And a toothbrush.

JACK REACHER BOOKS IN ORDRE OF PUBLICATION

Killing Floor(1997) ISBN-13: 9780553826166

This is where it all kicks off. Killing Floor introduces us to Jack Reacher, and straight away we get the basics: he's ex-military police, no fixed address, and travels the U.S. with the bare minimum—a fold of cash and a toothbrush. No phone, no luggage, no problem. He steps off a Greyhound bus in the small town of Margrave, Georgia, for no particular reason except he'd heard a blues musician once mentioned it. Within an hour, he's arrested for murder. Classic Reacher luck.

The book is a mixture of small-town paranoia, brutal conspiracies, and some very crunchy action. There's a counterfeiting operation bubbling underneath the surface, and pretty soon bodies start stacking up. Along the way, Reacher finds out something personal is tangled in all this—his older brother Joe (who worked for the U.S. Treasury) is also caught up in it. Reacher being Reacher, that's more than enough to make things personal.

What makes Killing Floor stand out is how fully formed

the whole thing is right from the beginning. Reacher arrives on the page with a voice that's confident, calm, and always a little bit detached. Lee Child's writing is clipped and to the point—short sentences, no fat—which perfectly matches the mood. There's a noir feel to it, but it's also got that big, bruising American thriller energy.

It's a strong debut and sets the tone for everything that comes after: justice delivered with a straight face and a clenched fist.

Die Trying(1998) ISBN-13: 9780553811889

Jack Reacher, minding his own business as usual, walks down a street in Chicago, offers to help a woman with a crutch, and next thing he knows—bang—he's bundled into the back of a van by armed men. Kidnapped. That's a proper Tuesday for Reacher. The woman, it turns out, is FBI agent Holly Johnson, and she's not just anyone—she's got connections right to the top. Unfortunately, their captors don't know (or care) about any of that. They've got a plan, and Reacher's now part of it, like it or not.

The story takes a sharp turn into the world of militias and isolated extremist compounds. The pair are dragged deep into the Montana wilderness, where a hard-line survivalist group is building a little empire of its own—off-grid, heavily armed, and very suspicious of outsiders. They've got a hostage plan that's politically explosive, and Holly's central to it. Reacher? He's just inconvenient. So naturally, he becomes a very big problem for them.

This book widens Reacher's world considerably. While Killing Floor was more contained and personal, Die Trying ups the stakes and introduces a more political edge. We see more of Reacher's military instincts—how he observes, calculates, and stays two steps ahead—and there's a growing sense that he's not just lucky; he's dangerous because he understands pressure. He's calm in chaos.

The chemistry between Reacher and Holly is sharp without being cheesy, and the pacing never lets up. It's tense, explosive, and properly satisfying.

Tripwire(1999) ISBN-13: 9780553811902

In Tripwire, Reacher's doing something almost shockingly normal—digging swimming pools in Key West. He's keeping things low-key, anonymous, sun-tanned, and dusty. That lasts all of five minutes. A private investigator turns up looking for him, gets himself killed before Reacher even knows why, and suddenly our man is on a flight to New York with questions that only seem to get uglier the deeper he digs.

This one's all about old ghosts. The trail leads to the widow of his old commanding officer, and a deeply unsettling mystery involving a missing soldier, dodgy identities, and someone doing very nasty things to veterans. There's also a truly sinister villain—Hook Hobie, a Wall Street fraudster with a prosthetic hand and absolutely no morals. Hobie is one of the great early Reacher baddies: intelligent, ruthless, and completely lacking a reverse gear. The showdown between him and Reacher is the stuff of legend—clever, brutal, and properly earned.

What really stands out in Tripwire is how it begins to explore Reacher's emotional landscape a bit more. He's not just a walking fist; there's regret, loyalty, and a deep respect for people who served and were forgotten. We also meet Jodie Garber, the daughter of Reacher's former CO, and there's a rare bit of romantic development that actually feels earned and human.

Tonally, it's darker and more emotional than the first two, but still packed with the kind of action that makes you want to punch a filing cabinet. Top-tier early Reacher.

Running Blind / The Visitor(2000) ISBN-13: 9780553811919

This one kicks off with Jack Reacher living a semi-domesticated life in New York with Jodie, the lawyer from *Tripwire*. He's got a house. He's buying groceries. He's even doing a bit of furniture shopping, which is very un-Reacher. Of course, it can't last. The FBI comes knocking, and suddenly he's being accused of murdering women he's never met. That's the hook—someone's killing women who once filed sexual harassment claims within the military system. There's no forced entry, no signs of struggle, and the crime scenes are eerily pristine. The FBI can't figure it out. But the killer clearly knows Reacher's past, and the timing's too sharp to be coincidence.

What follows is part mystery, part manhunt, part mind game. Reacher is dragged into helping the Bureau—mainly because they won't take no for an answer—and we get a lot more of his analytical side. He's a chess player in a world of blunt instruments, and here, that really shines. He starts building the profile, chasing patterns, and trying to work out who could be targeting him so personally.

The villain here is slippery and disturbing, and the final twist is a belter. It's not the most action-heavy Reacher novel, but it's full of dread and clever turns, with a real sense of ticking-clock tension. We also get more insight into how Reacher sees his military past, the compromises of the system, and his reasons for walking away.

It's a bit different, and that's what makes it work.

Echo Burning(2001) ISBN-13: 9780553813432

Reacher's out in Texas, hitchhiking through the desert heat and trying not to get arrested again—which, for him, is a full-time job. He gets picked up by a woman named Carmen Greer, who's in a right state: scared, bruised, and desperate.

She's convinced her abusive husband is about to be released from prison, and she thinks the only solution is to kill him before he kills her. So she's driving around West Texas, looking for someone dangerous and off the grid. Reacher ticks both boxes.

Naturally, Reacher doesn't just say "yes" to murder, but something about Carmen's situation doesn't sit right. He ends up back at her ranch, where the heat is oppressive, the family are strange, and the tension builds like a thunderstorm. When the husband does return, and a body turns up, things spiral fast. Reacher's drawn into a complex mess involving racial prejudice, buried secrets, and a legal system that's far too cosy with power.

This book stands out because it feels almost like a modern Western. There's the isolated ranch, the border town atmosphere, and the constant simmering danger of the sun-scorched landscape. Reacher's still dishing out justice, but this time it's more about patience, investigation, and unpicking layers of lies.

It's also one of the books where you see just how much he hates bullies—especially the kind who hide behind money, family, or law. There's action, of course, but this one's all about slow tension, psychological pressure, and watching Reacher unravel a truly nasty knot.

Without Fail(2002) ISBN-13: 9780553813449

In Without Fail, Jack Reacher gets a very unusual offer: help the U.S. Secret Service prevent the assassination of the Vice President–elect. Not stop a real threat—just test the defences. A red team job. Break into the system and show them where the cracks are. It's suggested by M.E. Froelich, a former army colleague of Reacher's late brother Joe, who now works security detail. Reacher agrees, partly out of curiosity, partly out of loyalty to Joe's memory, and partly because, well, who wouldn't want to legally poke holes in the most guarded person in America?

But what starts as a theoretical exercise very quickly turns real. A credible threat emerges, letters with chilling specifics start turning up, and suddenly Reacher's not just pointing out flaws—he's plugging them with his fists. It becomes a race against time to figure out who's behind the threat, what they really want, and how far they're willing to go.

This one feels tighter, more cerebral than some of the earlier books. It's less about wandering into trouble and more about precision: surveillance, strategy, reading behaviour. You see Reacher's military mind at full stretch, planning like a general, moving like a street brawler, and always ten steps ahead.

There's also a hint of romance that's handled with a surprisingly light touch, and Froelich's character adds both emotional weight and professional tension. It's a Reacher book with a suit-and-tie edge—but don't worry, there's still plenty of thumping where needed.

Persuader(2003) ISBN-13: 9780553815856

Persuader kicks off with a bang—Reacher "kills" a federal agent in broad daylight and bundles a young man into a car. Except, of course, it's all a setup. Reacher's working unofficially with the DEA, infiltrating a private fortress of a man named Zachary Beck, a suspected smuggler with links to a major criminal enterprise. But for Reacher, this mission is personal. One of Beck's associates is Francis Xavier Quinn, a brutal former military op Reacher thought he'd killed ten years earlier. Turns out he didn't finish the job—and that's not something Reacher can let slide.

So begins the most covert Reacher mission yet. He embeds himself as Beck's new hired muscle, slipping into a world of private guards, fortified homes, and a teenager who may be more vulnerable than anyone realises. What follows is an intense, slow-burn game of cat-and-mouse with violent payoffs, shady business dealings, and Reacher constantly walking a knife-edge between discovery and disaster.

There's a claustrophobic tension throughout—Reacher's in close quarters, can't trust anyone, and every move he makes could get him killed. But he's calm, methodical, and utterly unshakeable. The action scenes are some of the most brutal in the series, and the personal vendetta gives everything extra heat.

It's darker, bloodier, and more psychologically intense than the earlier books. Reacher's not just dispensing justice—he's out to correct a mistake. And when Reacher sets his sights on unfinished business, you know it's going to end with someone getting properly wrecked.

The Enemy(2004) (2004)ISBN-13: 9780553815856

The Enemy takes us back to 1990—Reacher's a major in the U.S. Military Police, stationed in North Carolina, and still officially part of the machinery. It's New Year's Eve, the Berlin Wall's just come down, and the world's in flux. Reacher's called in to investigate the death of a two-star general found dead in a seedy motel. No obvious foul play... but no obvious reason for him to be there either. Things get murkier when the general's briefcase goes missing and his wife is found murdered. Suddenly, it's not just about one dead man—it's about who he was, what he knew, and what someone's trying very hard to hide.

This is a slower, more procedural Reacher story. It's a military whodunnit wrapped in political manoeuvring, backstabbing, and a crumbling Cold War backdrop. Reacher's got rank, but not much support—his instincts are sharp as ever, but here he has to navigate brass, bureaucracy, and the thin line between orders and justice.

There's also a personal thread. Reacher's mother is ill, and he's grappling with the shifting shape of his own future. We get a rare glimpse of Reacher's family—especially his relationship with his older brother Joe—and hints of the disillusionment that eventually leads him to walk away from it all.

The Enemy shows us a younger Reacher, but no less determined. He's already the kind of man who digs until he finds the truth—no matter who's trying to bury it.

One Shot(2005) ISBN-13: 9780553815863

One Shot starts with a sniper. Six shots. Five dead. Clean, clinical, and seemingly random. The police move fast, and within hours they've got a suspect: James Barr, a former army marksman with a sketchy past. The evidence is airtight—fingerprints, vehicle, ammo, the lot. Barr says just one thing: "Get Jack Reacher."

Enter Reacher, rolling into town as he so often does—alone, unannounced, and already suspicious. Turns out, he knows Barr. Years ago, he investigated him for a similar incident in the Gulf—one that didn't lead to charges but left Reacher deeply uneasy. So this time, Reacher's not here to help the defence. He's here to bury the man.

But then, as always, things don't add up. The more Reacher digs, the more the case starts to smell wrong—too neat, too simple. Before long, he's wrapped up in a plot that involves Russian gangsters, a terrifying fixer called The Zec, and a cover-up that stretches well beyond the local precinct.

One Shot is pure procedural thriller—tight pacing, sharp twists, and a central mystery that builds beautifully. Reacher's logic and military detective work are on full display here, and the action scenes are clean and cinematic without going over the top. There's also some good chemistry with the lawyer, Helen Rodin, and a few moments of dark humour to break the tension.

This one really captures what Reacher's about: justice, clarity, and breaking bad people's noses when words won't do.

The Hard Way(2006) ISBN-13: 9780553817492

Reacher's minding his business in a New York café—drinking coffee, staring out the window, enjoying the quiet—when he notices something odd. A man gets into a car and drives off. Nothing dramatic, just off somehow. The next day, Reacher learns that moment was the key to a kidnapping. A woman and her young daughter have been taken, and the ransom's already in motion.

Enter Edward Lane. Rich, controlled, ex-special forces, and head of a high-end private security outfit made up of former soldiers. Lane hires Reacher to help track down the kidnappers, recover his wife and stepdaughter, and do it quickly—money's not an issue. But as Reacher gets deeper into Lane's world, he starts to feel the chill. The men Lane surrounds himself with are dangerous, loyal, and just a bit too polished. Something about Lane's story doesn't ring true, and Reacher's gut starts telling him that maybe he's not working for the good guys.

This one's sleek and efficient—part investigation, part manhunt, all grit. It's also one of those books where Reacher starts pulling at a single thread, only to unravel a whole bloody jumper. The tension builds beautifully, with New York and then rural England providing contrasting backdrops to a twisting plot.

Lane's a great "grey area" character—commanding, persuasive, but slippery—and Reacher's slow realisation of what he's actually involved in makes for a properly tense ride. As always, once he sees the truth, the gloves come off.

Bad Luck and Trouble(2007) ISBN-13: 9780553817492

When a former member of Reacher's old Army unit turns up dead—dumped out of a helicopter in the middle of the desert—Reacher doesn't wait around. He's living off the grid, as usual, but when Neagley (a fellow ex-MP and one of the few people he actually likes) tracks him down with the bad news, he drops everything. Someone is targeting the elite squad Reacher once led, and that's the kind of thing he doesn't take lightly.

Soon, Reacher and Neagley are piecing the team back together—what's left of it—and trying to figure out who's killing their friends and why. The trail leads to a corrupt defence contractor, an embezzlement scheme, and a plot that stretches from Los Angeles to Las Vegas, with plenty of dodgy goings-on in between. And as the bodies pile up, Reacher gets properly furious. Which, let's face it, never ends well for the villains.

This one's a blast. It's got a bit of that Oceans Eleven team-up energy, with Reacher pulling in old contacts and using all the military tricks they perfected together. There's proper camaraderie here—flashbacks to their army days, unspoken loyalties, and a real sense of old scores being settled.

It also reminds you that while Reacher often works alone, he's lethal in a unit. Especially when the mission is personal. This is Reacher with backup, and that makes things very bad indeed for anyone on the wrong side.

Nothing to Lose(2008) ISBN-13: 9780553824414

This one's got a brilliantly simple premise. Reacher's walking west, just following the road, and stumbles across two neighbouring towns in Colorado: Hope and Despair. He arrives in Despair, tries to get a coffee, and is immediately told to leave. No reason. No crime. Just "get out of town." So naturally, Reacher decides to stay and find out what's going on.

From that moment on, it's classic outsider-vs-the-system stuff. Reacher digs in, asks questions no one wants to answer, and crosses paths with corrupt cops, a paranoid businessman, and an entire town that seems built around secrecy. There's a military connection buried deep in the foundations of Despair—an old base with something very wrong going on behind its fences. Reacher teams up (sort of) with a local police officer from Hope, and together they start unravelling a disturbing story involving missing people, corporate greed, and a cover-up that stretches far further than it should.

This book has a slower rhythm than some of the earlier entries, but it uses that space well—building mood, tension, and a sense of creeping danger. Reacher's thought process is centre stage here: how he spots lies, how he pressures people, how he knows when to punch and when to wait.

It's one of those books that plays out like a long standoff

in a Western, with Reacher standing in the dust, watching a town that's watching him right back. It's all about control, pressure, and how far you can push before someone breaks.

Gone Tomorrow(2009) ISBN-13: 9780553824698

We open with Reacher riding the New York City subway at two in the morning, mentally checking off the behavioural profile of a suicide bomber. It's methodical, tense, and very Reacher—he's running through a detailed mental list (he's seen the training slides, he knows the signs), and a woman in the carriage ticks every single box. By the time the train pulls into the next station, she's dead. Not by bomb—by her own hand. That's chapter one. From there, things only get messier.

Reacher's curiosity gets the better of him. He wants to know why she did it, who she was, and why no one seems to want him asking questions. His digging pulls him into a tangled mess of political secrets, ex-military spooks, a shady private security firm, and a very dangerous woman with links to Afghanistan and some serious blood on her hands.

This one moves fast. It's urban, it's layered, and it's got a real espionage flavour to it—almost a spy thriller in places, with Reacher navigating a world of false identities, surveillance, and very powerful people trying very hard to make sure the truth stays buried. But he just keeps pulling at the threads.

There's a standout villain here in Susan Mark's shadowy handler, and some genuinely shocking moments. It's also one of the more cerebral entries—Reacher's deductions are razor-sharp, and the moral murkiness is thick.

Bottom line? Gone Tomorrow is tense, intelligent, and extremely satisfying.

61 Hours(2010) ISBN-13: 9780553825565

This one starts, weirdly enough, with Reacher on a tour bus full of pensioners that crashes in a snowstorm. He ends up stranded in Bolton, South Dakota—a bleak, frozen town where the wind bites hard and trouble's brewing. There's a witness being protected, a biker gang lurking on the outskirts, and a police force that's badly overstretched. And in the middle of all that? One big ex-military drifter who just wants a warm coat and a cup of coffee.

But Reacher being Reacher, he gets involved. The town's police chief ropes him in to help guard the witness—an elderly librarian who saw something she shouldn't have—and soon he's up to his neck in a strange mix of meth dealers, a mysterious underground military bunker, and a very old Cold War secret. There's also a mysterious voice on the other end of the phone from the Pentagon, which adds a proper spy-thriller flavour to the whole thing.

The title refers to a countdown clock ticking down through the novel's final pages, which adds a brilliant sense of urgency. As the hours tick by, the danger ramps up, and by the time you reach the end, it's a full-on sprint. Then—bang—a last-page twist so bold it had fans yelling at the book.

It's a quieter, colder Reacher story in some ways, but the tension is electric, and the payoff is brilliant. Just don't expect closure—you'll need the next book for that.

Worth Dying For(2010) ISBN-13: 9780553828481

We pick up straight after 61 Hours. Reacher's battered,

stitched up, and still dealing with the fallout from South
Dakota, but he's barely through the door of a dingy motel
in Nebraska before trouble finds him again. A drunk doctor,
a badly beaten woman, and a town held in the grip of
the Duncan clan—a local family who run a tight, vicious
operation that looks like old-school farm logistics but smells
an awful lot like modern slavery.

Reacher gets involved when he hears about Eleanor
Duncan, the woman with the bruises. No one else is doing
anything about it, and that's all the invitation he needs. But as
he starts peeling back layers, he discovers the Duncans aren't
just domestic abusers—they're middlemen in something
much uglier involving missing girls, violent enforcers, and
shadowy connections to international crime rings.

There's something deeply satisfying about how Reacher
works through this one. He's not at full strength, but that
doesn't stop him—it just makes him more creative. There's
a real Western vibe to the whole thing: a stranger walks into
a corrupt town and starts dishing out justice, one punch at a
time.

It's violent, yes, but also thoughtful. Reacher's not just
hitting people—he's trying to right a wrong that's gone
unnoticed too long. And when you see the full picture of
what the Duncans are covering up, you'll be cheering him on
every step of the way.

The Affair(2011) ISBN-13: 9780553825503

Set in 1997, The Affair is the prequel that finally shows us
the moment Jack Reacher walks away from the U.S. Army for
good. He's still a military police major here, still technically in
the system, but he's already feeling the cracks. The story drops
him into Carter Crossing, Mississippi—a small town near

a secretive military base—where a young woman has been murdered under suspicious circumstances. The army wants it handled quietly, and Reacher's sent in under cover, told to observe and report. You can imagine how long that lasts.

What he finds is a town full of fear, a local sheriff who's far sharper than she lets on (and, naturally, drawn to Reacher), and a military command that's very keen to make the problem go away. The deeper he digs, the worse it gets—there's more than one body, and the suspect list includes highly protected personnel. Reacher has to choose between his loyalty to the army and his personal sense of justice, and it's no spoiler to say which side he comes down on.

There's something very satisfying about watching Reacher transition from military man to drifter. You see him calculating the cost of staying, and the freedom of leaving. The mystery is taut, the politics are murky, and the final confrontation is classic Reacher—smart, fast, and devastating.

This one's not just a prequel—it's his origin story. The moment he becomes the man we meet in Killing Floor.

A Wanted Man(2012) ISBN-13: 9780553825534

We open with Reacher standing at a cloverleaf in Nebraska, hitchhiking west with a freshly busted nose and no particular destination. A car eventually stops—two men in the front, one woman in the back. They say they're on a business trip, heading for Chicago. But Reacher, despite the nasal swelling, can smell the weirdness immediately. The woman's tense, the men are evasive, and something is definitely off. He plays it cool, sits back, and starts quietly working out what they're really up to.

What follows is a cat-and-mouse thriller that stretches across several states and pulls in everything from a roadside murder to an FBI counterterrorism unit. Reacher, as usual, peels the situation apart with that calm, Sherlock-on-protein-shakes brain of his—observing, testing, and slowly shifting the odds in his favour.

The book is a slow burn at first, with much of the action playing out in conversations and mind games inside a moving car. But once the real threat becomes clear—and the FBI gets involved—it turns into something much bigger and faster. There's deception, danger, and a well-placed diner showdown, as always.

It's not quite as punch-heavy as earlier entries, but it's clever. Reacher's at his most calculating here, proving again that you don't need a gun when you've got a brain like a bear trap and fists like anvils. A slightly odd one, but oddly satisfying.

Never Go Back(2013) ISBN-13: 9780553825541

So here's the setup: Reacher, after roaming around in previous adventures, finally heads to Virginia to visit Major Susan Turner—the current commanding officer of the 110th MP unit he once led. They've spoken on the phone in earlier books, there's been a bit of spark, and now he's showing up in person. But when he arrives? Turner's gone. Arrested. And Reacher is very much not welcome.

Instead of a reunion, he's hit with two bombshells: he's being recalled to the army to face charges of a 16-year-old assault case, and, oh yes, he may have a teenage daughter he never knew about. It's all clearly a setup, but no one will say why—or who's behind it.

What follows is part fugitive thriller, part conspiracy unravel, and part Reacher road trip. He breaks Turner out of military custody, dodges a serious number of suits and goons, and digs into a conspiracy involving corrupt officers, military contractors, and the kind of behind-the-scenes politics that makes him very twitchy.

Reacher and Turner make a great team—there's chemistry, trust, and proper old-school military grit. The book moves fast, and the final showdown feels earned. There's also an unexpectedly touching subplot around the maybe-daughter, which brings a bit of introspection into Reacher's usually closed-off world.

It's Reacher vs. the system at full throttle. Dirty secrets, government heavies, and a strong sense that even when he tries to go back... it's never quite that simple.

Personal(2014) ISBN-13: 9780553828955

This time, the stakes are international. A sniper has taken a shot at the French president, from an impossible distance, and there are only a handful of people in the world who could've pulled it off. One of them is a man Reacher once put in prison—John Kott, a former American soldier, long-range shooting expert, and now off the radar.

The U.S. government wants Reacher to find him—quietly. They hand him a file, a phone, and an intelligence agent named Casey Nice, then point him towards Paris and London. It's a proper globe-trotter, and Reacher's not thrilled about the suitcases and hotels, but he's got a job to do, and it feels personal (hence the title).

The chase leads through embassies, criminal gangs, and shady diplomatic zones, but the real tension is in the sniper chess match. Reacher knows what Kott is capable of, and the book leans into the psychological game between two former military men who understand range, terrain, and patience better than most.

Casey Nice is a welcome sidekick—smart, sharp, and dealing with her own mental-health issues, which Reacher handles with surprising tact. There's plenty of action, of course, but also some lovely detective work and low-key dry humour.

Personal feels slicker and more espionage-flavoured than earlier books, and that's no bad thing. Reacher in Europe is still Reacher—observant, lethal, and very much the wrong man to cross.

Make Me(2015) ISBN-13: 9780857502674

Reacher steps off a train in a tiny, out-of-the-way town called Mother's Rest. It's the name that gets him—curious, strange, oddly poetic. He's not planning to stay long. But the town's quiet in all the wrong ways, and something feels very wrong underneath its sleepy surface.

He's approached almost immediately by Michelle Chang, a former FBI agent turned private investigator, who's looking for a colleague who's gone missing. The man was supposed to meet her in Mother's Rest—and then vanished. She mistakes Reacher for him at first, and once the confusion's cleared up, Reacher being Reacher, decides to help her anyway. Because a quiet town with no answers and someone gone missing? That's catnip for Jack Reacher.

What follows is one of the darkest investigations he's ever done. The plot stretches from dusty fields and empty motels to Silicon Valley and encrypted online communities, with a truly unsettling truth buried at the heart of it all. As Reacher and Chang dig deeper, they're met with silence, threats, and a conspiracy that's genuinely horrifying. And when the final reveal lands? It's one of the most shocking and bleakest moments in the entire series.

The chemistry between Reacher and Chang works well—they're both competent, unflinching, and determined. The pace is patient at first, then gradually builds until it explodes.

This is Reacher in detective mode, peeling back layers of something no one wants exposed. Brutal when it needs to be, compassionate when it matters, Make Me proves there are still stories that can surprise even Reacher.

Night School(2016) ISBN-13: 9780593073902

The year is 1996, and Reacher's just been given a medal for something we're not told about—typical—and instead of some well-earned downtime, he's sent straight to "school." But this is no normal training course. It's a covert inter-agency task force dressed up as a classroom. There's a CIA guy, an FBI agent, and Reacher, representing the military. The mission? Figure out what the hell's going on with a suspicious message intercepted in Hamburg: "The American wants a hundred million dollars."

So off he goes, pairing up with his old sergeant Frances Neagley (always a welcome presence—efficient, loyal, just as tough) and diving into the murky world of Middle Eastern arms dealers, rogue operators, and whispered meetings in foreign cities. The trail leads to a plot that could end in a catastrophic sale of nuclear material to very bad people—and Reacher's job is to stop it before the pieces fall into place.

The tone is very procedural—almost like a Le Carré thriller with more broken noses—and it's a slower burn than the modern Reacher novels, full of tradecraft, coded messages, and high-level deception. But it works, especially if you like watching Reacher play the long game.

There's a nice balance of action and cloak-and-dagger spy stuff, and seeing Reacher operate within the system—just before he decides to leave it forever—adds depth. He might be wearing the uniform, but you can feel him chafing against the rules.

The Midnight Line(2017) ISBN-13: 9780593078174

This one starts in the most Reacher way possible: he's walking through a town in Wisconsin, pops into a pawn shop out of idle interest, and spots a 2005 West Point class ring. Small, delicate, almost certainly a woman's. And immediately he knows—nobody gives up a ring like that unless they're in serious trouble. So he buys it. And sets off to find its original owner.

What unfolds is a slow, winding investigation that stretches from pawn shop to pill mill, touching on opioid addiction, missing veterans, and the kind of systemic failure Reacher can't ignore. The ring belonged to a woman named Serena Sanderson, and as Reacher follows the trail through South Dakota and Wyoming, he finds a world of people slipping through the cracks—injured vets, small-town addicts, crooked doctors. It's not flashy or high-stakes on the surface, but the human cost is enormous.

This is Reacher in full moral-crusader mode. He's quiet, methodical, deeply pissed off about the injustice, and absolutely determined to see it through. The action, when it comes, is clean and sharp—but it's the quieter moments that really land. His compassion for those forgotten by the system gives the book real weight.

It's slower-paced, for sure, but beautifully written, and arguably one of the most emotionally satisfying entries in the series. Proof, if it were needed, that Reacher doesn't need explosions to make an impact—sometimes, a pawned ring is all it takes.

Past Tense(2018) ISBN-13: 9780593078198

Reacher's on his usual wander when he sees a road sign: Laconia, New Hampshire—his father's hometown. On a whim, he decides to make a detour. He's not expecting much—maybe a gravestone, maybe a scrap of local history—but what he finds raises more questions than answers. According to local records, no one named Reacher ever lived there. Odd. And if there's one thing Jack Reacher doesn't let go of, it's "odd."

While Reacher starts sniffing around Laconia's dusty files and grumpy town officials, we're also following a second story: a young Canadian couple, Michaela and Shorty, who are road-tripping to New York but break down near a creepy, off-the-map motel. The owners are too friendly, the setting's too remote, and the vibe's all wrong. It starts off like a misadventure, but turns very dark, very quickly.

Of course, the two plots eventually converge. Reacher uncovers secrets about his own family that suggest things weren't quite as tidy as he thought, while Shorty and Michaela's story spirals into something deeply unsettling—like Deliverance with booking.com.

The dual structure works well here, with tension steadily rising on both sides. Reacher's sections are more investigative and nostalgic, while the motel storyline is pure claustrophobic thriller.

The tone's a bit more reflective than usual—Reacher's

legacy, family, identity—but rest assured, there's still plenty of tactical violence and righteous judgment. Because wherever Reacher goes, someone's always got it coming.

Blue Moon(2019) ISBN-13: 9781787633629

Reacher's on a bus—classic opening—when he notices an old man carrying a thick envelope of cash. Another passenger is watching him far too closely. So Reacher gets off the bus, follows the would-be thief, and interrupts what was about to be a nasty mugging. He gives the old man his envelope back and thinks that's the end of it. But this is Reacher, so of course it's not.

Turns out, the old man and his wife are in serious trouble—drowning in medical bills, targeted by loan sharks, and caught in a turf war between rival crime syndicates. One's Ukrainian, one's Albanian, and both are as unpleasant as you'd imagine. Reacher, naturally, takes this personally. What starts as a simple good deed turns into a one-man campaign against an entire city's worth of criminals.

The book is basically Reacher vs. organised crime, and the results are gloriously messy. He tears through corrupt bosses, hired killers, and assorted muscle with clinical efficiency, all while helping the old couple and uncovering a wider conspiracy involving international tech secrets. It's big, loud, and utterly shameless.

There's a Robin Hood energy to this one—Reacher handing out cash, righting wrongs, and walking away when it's done. Yes, the body count is ludicrous, and yes, some of it is a bit over the top—but it's all delivered with such style and momentum that you won't care.

Blue Moon is peak vigilante Reacher. It's not subtle, but it's an absolute ride.

The Sentinel(2020) ISBN-13: 9781787633612

The Sentinel marks a bit of a shift—Lee Child brings in his younger brother, Andrew Child (a.k.a. Andrew Grant), to co-write. The voice is a little different in places—quicker, slicker, maybe a touch more techie—but Reacher's still Reacher: big, blunt, and allergic to walking away when things look shady.

Reacher rolls into a town in Tennessee called Pleasantville, and as usual, it's anything but. He's barely unpacked his fists before he spots a man about to walk into a trap—an attempted kidnapping, in broad daylight, on a quiet street. Reacher steps in (of course), thumps the attackers, and rescues the man—Rusty Rutherford, an unassuming IT guy recently sacked after a cyberattack crippled the town's data systems. Rusty swears he's innocent. Reacher believes him. And when Rusty mentions the word "backups," everything suddenly kicks off.

It turns out this isn't just a local screw-up—it's tied to a much bigger plot involving hidden data, compromised systems, and a very modern sort of enemy. There are foreign agents, secret files, and some very shady local players who want Rusty silenced permanently. So Reacher becomes his bodyguard, his investigator, and, in a way, his avenger.

What's different here is the tech angle. There's a lot more digital espionage and online manipulation than usual, which feels like Andrew Child's influence coming through. That said, the heart of it is classic Reacher: identify the good guys, protect them, and flatten everyone else.

The tone is slightly breezier, the pace zippier, and the one-liners more frequent—but it still delivers the goods. If The Sentinel is the start of a new chapter, it's a solid one.

Better Off Dead(2021) ISBN-13: 9781787633735

Reacher's walking—surprise!—through a dusty town near the U.S.–Mexico border when he sees a crashed car on the side of the road. Inside: a woman named Michaela Fenton, unconscious, armed, and clearly dangerous. Turns out she's ex-FBI, on a desperate search for her missing twin brother. She thinks he's fallen into the hands of a mysterious figure known only as Dendoncker—a ghostlike crime boss who operates in the shadows and whose name strikes fear into just about everyone nearby.

As Reacher gets involved, he finds himself up against heavily armed goons, encrypted communications, abandoned warehouses, and the sort of violence that suggests Dendoncker isn't just running drugs—he's up to something much worse. The more he digs, the more the bodies pile up, and the deeper Michaela is dragged into something personal and very dangerous.

This one's got a stripped-back, noirish feel. It's set mostly at night, in claustrophobic buildings and desolate roads. Reacher's at his most relentless—calm, calculating, and absolutely merciless once he realises what kind of people he's dealing with. The action is brutal, the dialogue snappy, and the moral lines are drawn in thick, dark strokes.

There's less team-up work this time—Michaela's tough, but this is Reacher on a solo rampage for justice. The tone? Angry. The ending? Explosive. A rough ride, but a proper Reacher outing.

No Plan B(2022) ISBN-13: 9781787633759

It all kicks off in Gerrardsville, Colorado. Reacher sees a woman pushed in front of a bus. The police call it suicide. Reacher, having actually witnessed it, knows it was murder. And he knows the man who did it—but by the time he gets to the body and the scene, the man's vanished and the narrative's already been written.

So begins a cross-country chase to uncover the truth behind the murder, which is quickly tied to a shady prison facility called Minerva. On the surface, it's a cutting-edge rehabilitation centre. Underneath? Well, let's just say there's some very dodgy business going on involving blackmail, illegal adoptions, and a suspiciously efficient way of making people disappear.

The book juggles multiple points of view—something that started creeping in with the Andrew Child co-authorship. There's a grieving father, a runaway teen, and a corrupt administrator, all gradually spiralling into Reacher's orbit. Some readers love the broader scope, others miss the tighter, Reacher-only focus—but it does build into a satisfying payoff.

Reacher is in full moral fury mode here. Once he figures out what Minerva's really doing, he goes through the operation like a wrecking ball. It's got all the classic ingredients: the lone hero, the corrupt system, the sharp justice. If Better Off Dead was a brutal crawl through the dark, No Plan B is Reacher turning the lights on and taking names.

The Secret (2023) ISBN-13: 9781787633773

The year is 1992. Reacher's still in the army—still a major, still in the Military Police—and he's suddenly summoned to Washington for a job he doesn't want, by people who won't explain what's going on. All they'll say is: "Something's happening. We need you to look at it." Classic shadowy government vibes.

What's happening, it turns out, is that people with high-level security clearances are dying under mysterious circumstances—seemingly unconnected, but all within a short time frame. Natural causes, suicides, accidents... except they're not. And Reacher, being Reacher, spots the pattern. He's teamed up with a civilian FBI analyst named Julia Lam, and together they start unpicking a trail of corruption, fear, and something that reaches uncomfortably close to the highest levels of government.

The mood is very cloak-and-dagger. You get long nights in Washington offices, coded messages, hidden motives, and a real sense that Reacher is in a system designed to keep people quiet. But that's never stopped him before.

There's less open combat in this one, but more tension. Reacher's using his brain as much as his fists, playing the long game while still dishing out the occasional blunt-force solution when words run out. Lam is a solid sidekick—smart, composed, and refreshingly no-nonsense.

The Secret is about control, information, and the cost of silence. It's smart, sharp, and full of the slow, deliberate menace of a fuse burning down. A reminder that Reacher doesn't just bust heads—he also knows exactly when to wait, listen, and then pounce.

Jack Reacher wakes up in darkness, handcuffed to a bed, with a broken arm and no memory of how he got there. His last recollection is hitching a ride that ended in a fatal crash.

His captors, mistaking him for an accomplice, plan to extract information from him—a plan destined to backfire.

The narrative unfolds in the Ozarks, where Reacher becomes entangled with a criminal crew led by Darren Fletcher. The group is involved in art forgery, high-end burglary, and cyber-espionage. Reacher, seeking justice for the deceased driver, infiltrates the crew, navigating a web of deceit and betrayal.

He partners with Jenny Knight, a suspended Arizona detective seeking vengeance for her father's murder by one of Fletcher's associates. Together, they unravel a conspiracy involving stolen state secrets and a USB drive containing sensitive information. The plot thickens as Reacher confronts internal betrayals within the crew and external threats from those wanting the secrets kept buried.

The novel explores themes of memory loss, identity, and the moral complexities of justice. Reacher's physical limitations add a layer of vulnerability, but his determination remains unwavering. The story culminates in a high-stakes confrontation, with Reacher ensuring that those responsible face the consequences.

In Too Deep delivers the action and intrigue fans expect, while delving deeper into Reacher's psyche and the challenges he faces as he continues his solitary journey.

Exit Strategy (2025) ISBN-13: 9781787636880

Reacher's latest starts, as they often do, with something small: a coffee shop in Baltimore, a quiet drink, and a moment of idle people-watching. Then a young man brushes past him on the way out. Nothing dramatic. Until Reacher finds a handwritten note slipped into his pocket—urgent, scrawled, and unmistakably asking for help.

That's the hook, and Reacher, being who he is, doesn't ignore it. He wants to know who the young man is, why he was targeted, and what kind of mess he's just been nudged into. The trail quickly leads to something much larger and nastier than expected—a maze of secrets, surveillance, and people desperate to stay in the shadows.

The title, Exit Strategy, seems to hint at more than just Reacher's usual drop-in, blow-it-up, walk-away method. This time, there's a quiet tension from the start, with hints of government cover-ups, betrayal, and a larger chessboard in play. Reacher's never been big on subtlety, but he's smart enough to know when something doesn't add up—and patient enough to wait until it does.

Release date is Novemeber 2025.

Jack Reacher Books in Chronological order

The Enemy (2004)
The Secret (2023)
Night School (2016)
The Affair (2011)
Killing Floor (1997)
Die Trying (1998)
Tripwire (1999)
Running Blind / The Visitor (2000)
Echo Burning (2001)
Without Fail (2002)
Persuader (2003)
One Shot (2005)
The Hard Way (2006)
Bad Luck and Trouble (2007)
Nothing to Lose (2008)
Gone Tomorrow (2009)
61 Hours (2010)
Worth Dying For (2010)
A Wanted Man (2012)
Never Go Back (2013)
Personal (2014)
Make Me (2015)
The Midnight Line (2017)
Past Tense (2018)
Blue Moon (2019)
The Sentinel (2020)
Better Off Dead (2021)
No Plan B (2022)

In Too Deep (2024)
Exit Strategy (2025)

PUBLICATION ORDER OF JACK REACHER SHORT STORIES

Second Son (2011) ISBN-13: 9780857500106

This one takes us way back—Reacher as a teenager. A proper origin story in miniature, and a rare glimpse of what he was like before the toothbrush-and-army-jacket phase. We're in 1974, on a U.S. military base in Okinawa. Reacher's just 13, but already huge, already observant, and already a bit of a blunt instrument when it comes to solving problems.

The story kicks off with his father, Stan Reacher, receiving a troubling message from command—something to do with a top-secret security breach. Meanwhile, young Reacher's older brother, Joe, is tangled up in school trouble, and their mother is facing serious health issues. It's a lot, but young Reacher starts poking around and, naturally, ends up unravelling the real story behind the base's troubles.

It's short, but it packs a lot in. You see the early signs of the man he'll become—his instinct for justice, his sense of control under pressure, and that unflinching belief that you don't walk away when something's wrong. Even at 13, he's already the kind of lad who asks the right questions and doesn't wait for permission.

There's also a lovely moment where he stands up to a school bully in spectacular fashion—because of course he does.

It's not an action thriller, but it's a compelling little tale that adds depth to the Reacher mythos. A great bonus read for fans who want to know where it all started.

Deep Down (2012) ISBN-13: 9780857501042

Set in 1986, Deep Down features Reacher in uniform, posted to the Pentagon, and knee-deep in political landmines. He's been called in to quietly sniff out a leak—classified information about a new weapons system is being passed to foreign powers, and the suspects have been narrowed down to four female officers. Reacher's task is to get close, figure out who's behind it, and stop the flow—quietly, with no public fallout. Easy, right?

It's not your typical Reacher tale of bar fights and broken noses (though there's still some of that, don't worry). This one's more of a slow, cerebral job—observe, deduce, manipulate. Reacher's using his brain more than his fists, and the story moves at a satisfying investigative pace. He mingles, listens, plays dumb, and slowly zeroes in on the truth.

What's interesting is that the story plays with gender dynamics and assumptions. The Pentagon in the '80s wasn't exactly a hotbed of gender equality, and Reacher knows it. He uses the system's biases to his advantage—not to exploit, but to expose.

The final twist is nicely done, and it's one of those satisfying moments where Reacher doesn't need to throw a single punch to win—he just calmly backs someone into a corner with logic and a steely stare.

For a short story, Deep Down packs in a proper plot and offers a tidy slice of pre-drifter Reacher. Well worth the read, especially if you enjoy seeing him operate from the inside out.

High Heat(2013) ISBN-13: 9781473508887

It's July 1977. Reacher is 17, wandering the streets of New

York, waiting to catch a bus to a military academy. It's sweltering—one of those summer days where the city feels like it's on the verge of combustion. And it is, quite literally, about to go dark. The infamous NYC blackout is just hours away.

Before that happens, Reacher stumbles across two things: a woman in danger, and a dead body. The woman's being threatened by a shady man with mob connections. The body belongs to a murder victim whose case is being ignored by local cops. Naturally, Reacher—still growing into his full Reacher-ness but already full of righteous fury—decides to intervene.

What follows is a tight, noirish tale with a great ticking-clock vibe. You get young Reacher playing detective, challenging mobsters, befriending a sharp young journalist, and basically being the world's most terrifying teenager. And when the lights go out and the city erupts in chaos, he uses it to his full advantage.

There's a strong coming-of-age undercurrent here. Reacher is still learning, still shaping his code, but already dead certain about one thing: you stand up for what's right, no matter the odds.

Fast-paced, smart, and filled with noir energy, High Heat is a perfect bite-sized Reacher experience—moody, stylish, and absolutely roasting.

Not a Drill(2014) ISBN-13: 9781473508894

Reacher's wandering through Maine when he spots a noticeboard calling for volunteer hikers. Not exactly his thing, but the idea of clean air, trees, and no one trying to kill him is mildly appealing. So off he goes with a small group into the deep forest—three tourists, one guide, and Reacher with his usual curiosity and combat boots.

But this is no ordinary walking tour. The group is halted by a sudden military-style roadblock, the kind that's full of polite explanations and not-so-polite automatic rifles. Locals say it's all a routine drill. Reacher, being Reacher, doesn't buy it for a second.

When one of the tourists goes missing and the military presence starts looking more like a cover-up, Reacher starts digging. What he uncovers is a situation involving a rogue soldier, buried secrets, and the sort of quiet threat that could spiral into a national scandal. There's a definite eco-thriller undertone here—military land, indigenous concerns, hush-hush agendas—and Reacher cuts right through it all with that slow, relentless logic of his.

Not a Drill isn't as punchy as the novels, but it's got a tight mystery, a ticking-clock feel, and a satisfying unravel. It's also nice to see Reacher navigating a civilian situation before he inevitably turns it into a very non-civilian one.

Good and Valuable Consideration: Jack Reacher vs. Nick Heller(2014)

Originally published in FaceOff, no standalone ISBN

Good and Valuable Consideration isn't your average Reacher tale. It's a crossover short story—a face-off between two thriller heavyweights: Jack Reacher and Nick Heller (created by author Joseph Finder). Think of it as a literary sparring match with egos, ethics, and a bit of flexing from both sides.

Set entirely in a New York bar, this story is basically two blokes walking into a pub—but instead of a joke, it's a tension-fuelled debate about justice, ethics, and what to do when someone rich and powerful needs protecting from something they arguably deserve.

Nick Heller is on the job. He's been hired to provide security for a controversial CEO who's been making enemies left, right, and centre. Reacher's there because, well, he's Jack Reacher and doesn't need a reason to be anywhere. The two end up at the same table and find themselves debating the finer points of right and wrong.

There's no violence, no chase scenes—just two highly trained professionals with completely different methods trying to work each other out. It's clever, talky, and a bit philosophical, with a simmering tension beneath the surface.

It's less "Reacher breaks someone's arm with a sugar shaker" and more "Reacher calmly explains why someone probably needs punching." Think of it as a bottle episode in a thriller series: low-key, but quietly satisfying.

Small Wars(2015) ISBN-13: 9781473540484

Set in 1989, Small Wars drops us into the dying days of Reacher's army career. He's still a major in the Military Police, patrolling stateside bases and snapping salutes, but his instincts are already pulling him toward lone-wolf territory. The story begins when a promising young officer—Lieutenant Colonel Caroline Crawford—is found shot dead in her car on a remote Georgia road. It looks professional: two to the chest, one to the head. Cold, clean, and deeply suspicious.

Reacher is assigned to investigate, and he brings in trusted ally Frances Neagley to help him pick through the ranks. They're joined, interestingly, by Reacher's older brother Joe—still alive and well at this point, working Pentagon intelligence. The investigation takes them through layers of military politics, bitter rivalries, and the kind of secrets that ruin careers. And of course, there's a twist in the tail—one that makes the title feel particularly pointed.

This story sits just before The Enemy in the Reacher timeline, and it fills in some interesting background. You see Reacher still trying to play by the rules, but already becoming frustrated with the army's obsession with optics over truth.

It's tight, well-paced, and satisfyingly punchy—both in tone and in the occasional bout of actual punching. A perfect example of how Reacher doesn't need 400 pages to get to the bottom of things—and when he does, he never lets the guilty walk away clean.

Too Much Time(2017) ISBN-13: 9781473540491

Reacher's wandering through a small town in Maine, killing time and minding his business, when he sees a snatch-and-grab robbery—a bloke on a bike swipes a woman's purse. Reacher steps in with his usual surgical precision: one tackle, one collar, problem solved. The police arrive, impressed and grateful... for about five minutes. Then they ask him to stick around and give a statement.

That's where things go sideways.

Reacher gets arrested. Not for the tackle—but for being part of the crime. It's nonsense, obviously, but the more he looks into it, the more he realises the whole thing's a setup. And not just a petty stitch-up either. This is part of something organised, deliberate, and sinister. A conspiracy rooted in the local justice system, with ties to darker operations beyond the town limits.

What starts as a good deed turns into a twisting investigation, with Reacher doing what he does best—quietly dismantling a corrupt setup one piece at a time, and occasionally dropping people who really deserve it.

It's a modern Reacher tale: lean, smart, and full of that "don't poke the bear" energy. He might not be in uniform anymore, but the instincts are still there—and so is the moral compass, firmly pointed at justice.

Too Much Time also acts as a kind of teaser for The Midnight Line, but it stands strong on its own as a classic "wrong man in the wrong place" story—except Reacher's never quite the wrong man.

The Christmas Scorpion(2018) ISBN-13: 9781473563544

Reacher's in England this time—Norfolk, specifically. It's Christmas Eve, and he's holed up in a country pub trying to escape the cold. It's blowing a blizzard outside, but Reacher's just after a pint, a plate of food, and as little conversation as possible. Naturally, none of that goes to plan.

Two people arrive—American agents, clearly on edge. They're guarding a U.S. diplomatic figure staying in the area, and they've had word that an assassin has infiltrated the village. The killer's code name? The Scorpion. Their plan's falling apart fast, the snowstorm has wrecked comms, and they need help. Reacher being Reacher, he doesn't exactly volunteer—but he also doesn't like the idea of an assassin running loose at Christmas.

The entire story takes place in one location—one room, really—but it still manages to build tension. It's a neat little whodunnit with a spy-thriller edge. Reacher sizes everyone up, keeps his observations to himself, and starts quietly deducing who's legit and who's faking it.

There's a lovely moment where he uses pure logic and pressure to unmask the assassin—no gadgets, no guns, just

Reacher's ability to read people like instruction manuals.

At under 15 pages, it's a brisk read, but a satisfying one. Proof, if you needed it, that Reacher doesn't need a city or a war zone to sort things out—just a pub, a problem, and someone worth protecting.

Cleaning the Gold(2019) ISBN-13: 9780008355780

Jack Reacher heads to Fort Knox. Not for the gold, mind—but because someone once told him a long-ago murder happened there. A soldier died, the case went cold, and now Reacher wants to poke the ashes. Just a quiet look around. Of course, nothing is ever that simple.

Will Trent is also at Fort Knox—undercover, posing as part of the cleaning crew. He's investigating a separate case involving corruption, cover-ups, and a serious security breach. When he spots Reacher nosing about, he assumes he's trouble. And Reacher, being Reacher, assumes the same about Trent.

What follows is a taut little two-hander: two investigators, two conflicting missions, and a slowly unfolding realisation that they might—just might—be on the same side. The setting is sharp: Fort Knox's high-security, high-stakes atmosphere adds constant tension, and the gold vault itself becomes a kind of pressure cooker. Everyone's watching everyone else, and trust is in very short supply.

There's not loads of action, but when it comes, it's swift and brutal. What really makes this story sing is the contrast between Reacher's quiet physical presence and Trent's more methodical, psychological approach. They're very different blokes, but both want the same thing: justice, preferably delivered with finality.

It's a clever little novella—more about mood, mistrust, and professional tension than flying fists—but it's well worth it. A fun one-off that shows what happens when two different kinds of lone wolf cross paths in a den of secrets.

New Kid in Town (2024) ISBN-13: 9798874809157

New Kid in Town is the latest Reacher short story, penned solo by Andrew Child and released in April 2024. It originally appeared in the anthology Hotel California, with each story inspired by a track from the Eagles' classic album. This one riffs on "New Kid in Town," and it's pure Reacher: dusty roads, dodgy locals, and justice served with a side of menace.

Reacher's hitching his way across Texas when he lands in a sleepy backwater town that's got "trouble" written all over it. He's just looking for a ride and maybe a bite to eat, but as always, he finds himself in the middle of someone else's mess. This time, it's a family in danger and a criminal hiding in plain sight. Reacher steps in, and things escalate quickly.

The story is brief—just 38 pages—but it packs in the essentials: a mysterious stranger, a town with secrets, and Reacher's unerring sense of right and wrong. The action is swift, the dialogue sharp, and the atmosphere tense. It's a classic Reacher setup, distilled into a tight, punchy narrative.

Some readers have noted that the story feels more like a snapshot than a full narrative, with an abrupt ending that leaves a few threads hanging. But for fans of the series, it's a satisfying glimpse into Reacher's world—a reminder that wherever he goes, trouble follows, and he's always ready to face it head-on.

PUBLICATION ORDER OF JACK REACHER COLLECTIONS

Jack Reacher's Rules (2012) ISBN-13: 9780593070833

This one's pure fun—a quote-heavy guidebook compiled from the Reacher novels, laying out his personal rules, principles, and many, many thoughts on coffee, violence, travel, and not carrying anything you can't fit in your pockets.

It's not a story. There's no plot. It's part survival guide, part comedy, part distillation of Reacher's worldview. Some rules are serious: "Never volunteer for anything." Others are just delightfully blunt: "Get a bigger gun." There's practical wisdom too—how to fight dirty, travel light, and read a lie in someone's eyes. It's illustrated, smartly designed, and makes a great gift for die-hard fans or anyone with minimalist aspirations and strong opinions on hotel sheets.

Definitely not essential reading—but a good laugh, and a neat little tribute to one of fiction's most straightforward (and unbothered) heroes.

No Middle Name (2017) ISBN-13:

9780593079027

This is the definitive Jack Reacher short story collection—a
proper bookshelf beast that gathers almost all the Reacher
shorts into one place. It includes Second Son, Deep Down,
High Heat, Not a Drill, Small Wars, The Christmas Scorpion,
and Too Much Time, plus a few others that hadn't appeared
elsewhere before.

Among the exclusives is The Very First Reacher, which is
exactly what it sounds like—Reacher as a baby. Not a joke.
It's an odd little glimpse into the world before Reacher was
Reacher. Another standout is Everyone Talks, a rare story told
not from Reacher's perspective, but from someone who's
trying to figure out who this terrifying man is.

The tone shifts across the collection—from teenage
Reacher in Okinawa to military investigations, roadside
incidents, and off-the-grid encounters. Some are reflective,
others are straight-up brawls. It's not just bonus content—it's
a proper tour of Reacher's past lives, filled with the kind
of detail and texture you don't always get in the full-length
novels.

If you're a completist or just want bite-sized Reacher you
can read in one go, this is the collection to get.

Jack Reacher Quiz: 20 Questions

1. 1. In which US state is Killing Floor set?

2. What is the only item Jack Reacher regularly carries with him?

3. Which branch of the military did Reacher serve in?

4. What rank did Reacher hold before leaving the military?

5. What is the name of the woman Reacher helps in Echo Burning?

6. In The Midnight Line, what object does Reacher find in a pawn shop that sets the story in motion?

7. What is the name of the corrupt family Reacher confronts in Worth Dying For?

8. Which story is set during Reacher's teenage years and takes place during the 1977 New York blackout?

9. Which recurring character is known for her almost Reacher-level competence and used to serve under his command?

10. What's the title of the Reacher novel set almost entirely in the snow-covered town of Bolton, South Dakota?

11. Which short story is set entirely in one English pub

during a snowstorm on Christmas Eve?

12. In Personal, Reacher is tracking down which type of specialist assassin?

13. Which Reacher story involves a plot set within Fort Knox?

14. What's the name of the former military colleague Reacher goes to visit in Never Go Back?

15. Which Reacher book was the first to be co-written by Andrew Child?

16. What's the title of the prequel novel that shows Reacher just before he leaves the army?

17. What job is Rusty Rutherford wrongly blamed for messing up in The Sentinel?

18. Which book starts with Reacher witnessing a woman being pushed under a bus?

19. In Blue Moon, Reacher finds himself caught between which two feuding criminal factions?

20. What item of clothing does Reacher famously refuse to carry around?

JACK REACHER ON SCREEN: FROM MISCAST BLOCKBUSTER TO PRIME REDEMPTION

Jack Reacher walks into towns, not boardrooms. He solves problems with logic and elbows. He doesn't own a phone, rarely speaks more than necessary, and has all the social subtlety of a crowbar. So when Hollywood came calling, the big question was: how do you put a man like that on screen?

It turns out, you cast Tom Cruise. Twice.

And then, ten years later, you get it right.

This is the story of Jack Reacher's journey from page to screen—from controversial casting in slick blockbusters to near-universal praise in a streaming reboot that finally captured the man as Lee Child imagined him. And while no stage adaptation has ever made it to the West End or Broadway (yet), there's a theatricality to Reacher that makes him ripe for the boards, should someone be bold enough to try.

Let's start, inevitably, with Cruise.

THE TOM CRUISE ERA: TWO FILMS, BIG DIVIDE

Jack Reacher (2012)Released: 21 December 2012 (UK)Distributor: Paramount PicturesDirector: Christopher McQuarrie

In 2012, Tom Cruise—5'7" on a good day, Hollywood royalty, and eternally youthful—took on the role of Jack Reacher in a film adaptation of One Shot, the ninth Reacher novel. The internet was not pleased.

In the books, Reacher is described repeatedly as 6'5", 250 pounds, with hands like spades and a presence that makes rooms go quiet. Cruise, for all his intensity and acting chops, was physically the complete opposite. Lee Child publicly defended the casting at the time, saying Cruise captured the "essence" of Reacher. But fans felt otherwise. One particularly damning summary: "Reacher should tower. Cruise glowers."

Still, the film itself wasn't terrible. In fact, Jack Reacher (the film) did well enough with general audiences. Christopher McQuarrie directed a clean, well-paced thriller with a solid mystery at its heart, and Cruise, to his credit, leaned into the character's detached cool. The action was tight, the monologues sparse, and there was enough "Reacher logic" to keep things recognisable.

But the core issue lingered: Cruise wasn't Reacher. He was playing a man called Reacher. And that's not quite the same thing.

Jack Reacher: Never Go Back (2016)Released: 21 October 2016 (UK)Distributor: Paramount PicturesDirector: Edward Zwick

Four years later came Never Go Back, based on the 2013 novel of the same name. Cruise returned, joined by Cobie Smulders as Major Susan Turner. The plot followed Reacher as he tries to unravel a military conspiracy while also facing the possibility of a teenage daughter he never knew he had.

The tone here was more emotional, more personal, and frankly, more muddled. Critics were underwhelmed, and fans weren't thrilled either. The physical mismatch hadn't been fixed, and this time, the script didn't compensate.

It wasn't a disaster, but it was clear the Cruise experiment had run its course. Two films in, and the Reacher franchise felt adrift—profitable, maybe, but not true to the source. For fans, it was like watching a karaoke version of your favourite song. The words were there, the beat was fine, but the voice didn't match.

Lee Child, to his credit, acknowledged the problem. While he praised Cruise's performance, he later admitted: "Ultimately, the readers were right."

THE AMAZON PRIME SERIES: BACK TO BASICS, BACK TO REACHER

Reacher (TV series)Debut: 4 February 2022 (Season 1, Amazon Prime Video)Season 2: Released 15 December 2023Developed by Nick SantoraStarring: Alan Ritchson as Jack Reacher

Enter Amazon. Enter Alan Ritchson. Enter the actual Jack Reacher.

When Reacher debuted on Prime Video in 2022, it was like someone had finally opened the right file. Based on the very first Reacher novel, Killing Floor, the show starred Alan Ritchson—a former football player, properly huge, square-jawed, and just the right mix of physical menace and dry wit.

From the moment Ritchson stepped off the bus and ordered peach pie in Margrave, Georgia, the tone was right. This wasn't a slick action hero in sunglasses. This was a quiet giant with a moral compass, doing the maths in his head before delivering a precise headbutt.

Season one followed the Killing Floor plot closely: Reacher arrives in town, gets arrested for murder, and slowly unpicks a conspiracy involving counterfeit money, family secrets, and local corruption. It was faithful, well-paced, and full of what fans loved: clean logic, brutal fights, and that wonderfully Reacher-ish habit of noticing everything.

Season two, released in December 2023, adapted Bad Luck and Trouble. This time, Reacher reunites with former army colleagues to investigate the death of a teammate. The stakes were higher, the action more intense, and the team dynamics added warmth and humour.

Both seasons were hits. Critics praised the show's muscular storytelling and no-nonsense tone. Fans, especially long-time readers, were overjoyed. "Finally," they said, "this is our Reacher."

Amazon renewed the series quickly. Ritchson is now firmly established as the screen Reacher.

SEASON 3: A TITANIC RETURN TO FORM

Reacher Season 3Premiered: 20 February 2025 (Amazon Prime Video)Episodes: 8 (Weekly releases through 27 March 2025)Based on: Persuader (2003), the seventh novel by Lee Child

Season 3 of Reacher marks a significant milestone in the series, adapting Persuader, a fan-favourite novel that plunges Reacher into one of his most perilous undercover missions. This season sees Reacher attempting to rescue an undercover DEA informant, leading him into the dark heart of a criminal enterprise and confronting ghosts from his past.

Alan Ritchson returns as Jack Reacher, delivering a

performance that continues to embody the physicality and stoicism fans have come to expect. This season introduces Olivier Richters as Paulie, a towering adversary who presents a unique physical challenge for Reacher. Their confrontations are a highlight, showcasing intense choreography and palpable tension.

Season 3 delves deeper into Reacher's psyche, exploring themes of redemption and the lingering shadows of past decisions. The storyline is tightly woven, with each episode peeling back layers of the central mystery while maintaining the series' hallmark of suspense and action.

The third season has been met with acclaim, praised for its faithful adaptation of the source material and the continued evolution of its central character. The dynamic between Reacher and his allies, as well as the formidable new antagonist, has been highlighted as a standout aspect of the season.

With Season 3 solidifying Reacher's status as a flagship series for Amazon Prime Video, anticipation is already building for future instalments. The series continues to set a high bar for action thrillers, combining compelling storytelling with visceral action sequences.

WHY THE SERIES WORKS

The Prime show gets two things right.

First: casting. Ritchson isn't just tall—he acts tall. His stillness, his presence, the way he moves—all feel authentically Reacher. He's not flashy. He's confident but not cocky. And crucially, he never oversells it. He lets the character breathe.

Second: tone. The series embraces the simplicity of the books. There's mystery, sure, and plenty of world-building, but it's not padded with fluff. It trusts the source material.

Each season is eight episodes—tight, purposeful, and full of Reacher doing what Reacher does best: observing, investigating, and occasionally flooring someone with a single punch.

Even the dialogue feels right. No quippy Marvel-style banter. Just clipped, purposeful speech, loaded with Reacher's trademark understatement.

WHAT ABOUT THE STAGE?

So far, Jack Reacher has not made it to the theatre. There's no West End adaptation, no touring play, no solo monologue show titled Reacher: The Man Who Walked In. But it's not entirely ridiculous to imagine it.

Think about it. A stripped-back set. A diner booth. A motel room. A single chair and a pack of cards. Reacher monologues could work as theatre—dry, intense, and razor-sharp. The tension of a police interview. The ticking clock of a cover-up. A man alone on stage, explaining how he solved a murder using a coffee stain and a receipt.

There's definitely potential. But perhaps the reason we haven't seen it yet is that Reacher is so physical. His silence, his stature, the way he controls a room—these things don't always translate to the stage without the sheer presence of a massive actor to carry them. Still, if someone figures out how to stage it properly, it could be electric.

Until then, the screen will do.

THE REACHER FORMULA ON SCREEN

What ties all the adaptations together, whether successful or not, is the attempt to bottle what makes Reacher so compelling.

He's smart, but not showy.

He's violent, but never cruel.

He's kind, but emotionally untethered.

He doesn't chase power, but he is power.

On screen, these traits can be hard to capture. Too much emotion, and he seems soft. Too much silence, and he seems dull. Too much action, and you lose the moral weight. It's a balance—one Cruise came close to but never quite nailed, and one Ritchson seems to have instinctively understood.

Jack Reacher is not an easy character to adapt. He's part enigma, part moral compass, part blunt object. But when done right—as the Prime series proves—it's a joy to watch him work.

The Cruise films gave the character visibility and Hollywood sheen, but at the cost of authenticity. The Amazon series brought him home—big, bold, and beautifully true to the books.

And while the stage may never see Reacher stride across it, the idea isn't impossible. After all, if Shakespeare can write about revenge and justice using just a skull and a soliloquy, surely someone can do the same with a toothbrush and a coffee mug.

Until then, he'll keep walking—town to town, screen to screen, forever alone, forever observing, and forever ready to set things right.

Answers

1. Georgia

2. A toothbrush

3. Military Police

4. Major

5. Carmen Greer

6. A West Point class ring

7. The Duncan family

8. High Heat

9. Frances Neagley

10. 61 Hours

11. The Christmas Scorpion

12. A sniper

13. Cleaning the Gold

14. Major Susan Turner

15. The Sentinel

16. The Affair

17. A town's IT system

18. No Plan B

19. Albanians and Ukrainians

20. A suitcase

www.ingramcontent.com/pod-product-compliance
Lightning Source LLC
Chambersburg PA
CBHW050828250726

48653CB00006B/2487